MOUNTAIN CLIMBING

BY SARA GREEN

BELLWETHER MEDIA • MINNEAPOLIS, MN

Jump into the cockpit and take flight with Pilot books. Your journey will take you on high-energy adventures as you learn about all that is wild, weird, fascinating, and fun!

This edition first published in 2013 by Bellwether Media, Inc.

No part of this publication may be reproduced in whole or in part without written permission of the publisher. For information regarding permission, write to Bellwether Media, Inc., Attention: Permissions Department, 5357 Penn Avenue South, Minneapolis, MN 55419.

Library of Congress Cataloging-in-Publication Data

Green, Sara, 1964-
  Mountain climbing / by Sara Green.
    p. cm. – (Pilot: outdoor adventures)
  Includes bibliographical references and index.
  Summary: "Engaging images accompany information about mountain climbing. The combination of high-interest subject matter and narrative text is intended for students in grades 3 through 7"–Provided by publisher.
  ISBN 978-1-60014-892-7 (hardcover : alk. paper)
  1. Mountaineering–Juvenile literature. I. Title.
  GV200.G755 2013
  796.522–dc23
                                        2012037784

Printed in the United States of America, North Mankato, MN.

TABLE OF CONTENTS

A MOUNTAIN ADVENTURE

Several mountain climbers awake before dawn to bitter cold. They had spent the night in tents below the summit of Mount Everest, the world's tallest mountain. Today they will attempt the steep and difficult climb to the top.

The climbers use headlamps to see and bottled oxygen to breathe in the high altitude. They grip ropes bolted to the rocks on the steepest sections of the climb. Finally, after hours of climbing, they see the flags that mark the top of the mountain. At the summit, the climbers marvel at the view and pose for pictures. They are standing on the top of the world!

Everest

Mount Everest stands 29,035 feet (8,850 meters) tall and is located in Asia between Tibet and Nepal. On May 29, 1953, Edmund Hillary and Tenzing Norgay became the first people to summit Mount Everest.

Mountain climbing is an activity where people hike up or climb mountains. People go climbing for a variety of reasons. Many enjoy exploring new places and testing their limits. Some climbers participate in scientific research. They may study the plants, animals, or climate of the mountains. Photographers climb high to take pictures of spectacular mountain scenery.

Mountain climbing is for people of all ages and skill levels. The easiest climbs have marked trails. People can hike to the summit in a few hours. Difficult climbs require much skill and months of preparation. Climbers must know how to navigate ice, rock, and glaciers. They need strength and endurance to face great physical and mental challenges.

Many mountain climbers join **expeditions**. In these adventures, two or more people team together to climb mountains. They often travel long distances to mountain ranges far from populated areas. The Himalayan Mountains in Asia and the Andes Mountains in South America are two popular destinations.

Expeditions often last several days or even weeks. Because of this, they require a lot of gear. **Porters** and **pack animals** often help climbers carry their gear part of the way. Climbers set up a base camp before attempting the summit. Here, they rest and **acclimate** to the conditions.

GEAR UP FOR THE CLIMB

Mountain climbers must be prepared to handle difficult terrain, changing weather, and injuries. All climbers carry plenty of food and water. They also wear sturdy boots. Climbers usually dress in layers of warm, lightweight clothing. That way they can adjust to changes in temperature. Climbers should also wear hats, sunscreen, and sunglasses. They should always bring a basic first aid kit, matches, maps, and a compass.

oxygen

Expedition climbs require more equipment. Climbers need tents, sleeping bags, and sleeping pads for base camp. Many use small stoves for cooking food. Climbers often rely on water from natural sources. They carry water purifiers to make the water safe to drink. The air contains little oxygen at high altitudes. Many climbers carry bottled oxygen to help them breathe.

Climbers wear special gear to stay safe. Helmets protect their heads from falling rock and ice. Headlamps allow climbers to see in the dark. Rope has many useful purposes. Climbers string rope through their **harnesses** to attach themselves to one another. This helps them avoid falling or straying from the group. Climbers also use rope to **belay** one another.

Climbing on snow and ice has its dangers. Climbers attach spiked plates called crampons to the bottoms of their boots. Crampons help them travel on slippery surfaces. Many climbers carry ice axes. These long blades with teeth can be jammed into ice to aid climbing.

crampons

SAFE TO THE SUMMIT

Mountain climbers must be prepared to handle emergencies. Falling can cause severe injuries or death. Cold temperatures, blizzards, and high winds are common at high altitudes. They can lead to **hypothermia** and **frostbite**. Climbers can get lost in **whiteouts** and buried by **avalanches**. Thunderstorms can produce dangerous lightning. Climbers should seek cover at the first sign of a storm.

Altitude sickness affects many climbers. This condition brings on headaches, **nausea**, and dizziness above 6,000 feet (1,829 meters). It can also make breathing difficult for climbers. To avoid altitude sickness, climbers often spend a few days at high altitudes before beginning a climb. This allows them to acclimate. Climbing slowly with frequent rest stops also helps climbers avoid altitude sickness.

Eight Thousanders

The 14 highest mountain peaks tower more than 8,000 meters (26,247 feet) above sea level. People call them the "Eight Thousanders." All of them are located in the Himalayan and Karakoram ranges in central Asia.

Mountain climbing is less dangerous when climbers follow important safety guidelines. Climbing in groups is safer than climbing alone. In case of an emergency, a friend or family member should have details about the climbing trip. This includes the routes and climbing schedule. Climbers must also be willing to cancel their trip or cut it short if the weather is threatening.

Responsible mountain climbers respect rules and nature. They purchase special climbing permits for certain areas. They also avoid mountains that certain cultures consider sacred. Respectful climbers never leave a trace of their visit behind. All leftover food and trash is taken home.

Seven Summits

The Seven Summits are the highest mountains on each of the seven continents. Alaska's Mount McKinley is the highest mountain peak in North America. It stands 20,320 feet (6,194 meters) above sea level.

Mountain climbing is a great way to experience the outdoors. Many communities have hiking or mountain clubs that organize climbs. They also teach many of the skills that are needed for successful climbs.

Beginning climbers may prefer to climb with mountain guides. These expert mountain climbers teach skills and share knowledge about the environment. They also know how to handle emergencies. With the help of guides, many people have climbed above the clouds to reach spectacular summits.

CLIMBING MOUNT HOOD

Mount Hood is one of the most popular peaks in the world. Around 10,000 people climb this mountain every year. It stands 11,239 feet (3,426 meters) high in the Cascade Range near Portland, Oregon.

The best time of year to climb Mount Hood is in the spring. However, climbers should be prepared for cold, windy weather during any season. Beginners often enjoy hiking on the Timberline Trail. It crosses meadows and glacial creeks as it zigzags around the mountain. Advanced climbers can attempt more difficult routes to the top. Navigating steep rocks, ice walls, and glaciers is a challenge and a thrill!

Portland

Mount Hood

Oregon

N
W E
S

GLOSSARY

acclimate—to physically adjust to a new environment

altitude—the height above sea level

avalanches—large masses of falling snow, ice, or rock

belay—to tighten rope attached to another climber to keep him or her secure in case of a fall

compass—an instrument that shows the directions of north, south, east, and west

endurance—the ability to do something for a long time

expeditions—trips taken by groups of people for a specific purpose

frostbite—injury to body tissues exposed to extreme cold; frostbite most often affects the toes, fingers, nose, and ears.

glaciers—massive sheets of ice that cover a large area of land

harnesses—safety belts with leg loops

hypothermia—a condition in which one's body temperature is dangerously low

nausea—a feeling of wanting to throw up

pack animals—working animals that carry loads for people

permits—documents that give legal permission to do an activity

porters—people who carry gear for others

sacred—considered holy, or deserving of great respect and honor

sleeping pads—cushioned pads that provide comfort and protect campers from the cold ground

summit—the highest point of a mountain

terrain—a stretch of land

water purifiers—filters or tablets that remove unhealthy materials from water to make it safe to drink

whiteouts—blizzard conditions that make it impossible to see anything but snow; whiteouts can also occur in foggy conditions.

TO LEARN MORE

At the Library

Blanc, Katherine. *The Boy Who Conquered Everest: The Jordan Romero Story*. New York, N.Y.: Hay House, 2010.

Doeden, Matt. *Can You Survive Extreme Mountain Climbing? An Interactive Survival Adventure*. Mankato, Minn.: Capstone Press, 2013.

Kerr, Jim. *Hillary and Norgay's Mount Everest Adventure*. Chicago, Ill.: Heinemann Library, 2008.

On the Web

Learning more about mountain climbing is as easy as 1, 2, 3.

1. Go to www.factsurfer.com.

2. Enter "mountain climbing" into the search box.

3. Click the "Surf" button and you will see a list of related Web sites.

With factsurfer.com, finding more information is just a click away.

INDEX

The images in this book are reproduced through the courtesy of: Norbert Eisele-Hein Image Broker/Newscom, front cover, pp. 6-7; Dominik Michalek, pp. 1 (background), 8; AP Photo/ Hiroyuki Kuraoka, HO), pp. 4-5; Meigianbao, p. 9; Monkey Business Images, p. 10; Harry Kikstra/Getty Images, p. 11; AGENCE ZOOM/Getty Images, p. 12; David Trood/Getty Images, pp. 13, 15 (bottom); My Good Images, p. 15(top); Mike Meysner Photography/Getty Images, pp. 16-17; Stefan Petrovski, pp. 18-19; Danny Warren, p. 21 (top); Lonnie Gorsline, p. 21 (bottom).

MAR 2013